Things to Know Before Starting a Rental Real Estate Company

First published by Kjøller 2023

Table of Contents

Introduction

Real estate is a profitable industry, and one of the easiest ways to jumpstart your investment journey is by starting a rental real estate company. But while it may seem easy, there are various things you need to know before starting a rental real estate company. From understanding the basics to complex financial terms, this book is a comprehensive glossary containing essential information on everything you need to know to venture into the world of rental real estate. Whether you're an experienced investor or starting from scratch, this book is your roadmap to success in the rental real estate industry.

Accountant

An accountant is a professional who specializes in financial accounting and tax preparation. Starting a rental real estate company involves a variety of financial transactions, including property purchases, rental income, and expenses. Therefore, it is essential to work with an experienced accountant who can provide financial advice and ensure that all tax obligations are met.

Active Income

Active income refers to income generated from active participation in a business or job. This type of income is essential to consider when starting a rental real estate company because investors must decide if they will actively manage their rental properties or hire a property manager to do so, which can affect the amount of active income earned.

Amortization

Amortization is the process of paying off a loan over time through a series of fixed payments. This term is important to understand when starting a rental real estate company because loans are often used to finance the purchase of rental properties. Understanding amortization helps investors determine the monthly payments needed to pay off these loans over time.

Annual Gross Income

Annual Gross Income refers to the total income generated from rental properties in a year. When starting a rental real estate company, it is crucial to understand the concept of annual gross income because it is a prime factor in determining the profitability of rental properties.

Annual Percentage Rate (APR)

The Annual Percentage Rate (APR) is the cost of borrowing money expressed as a percentage rate over one year. This rate includes the interest rate, mortgage insurance, and other fees associated with borrowing money. This rate is important to consider when starting a rental real estate company because it affects the cost of financing the purchase of rental properties.

Appraisal

Appraisal is the process of determining the value of a property. Property values are important in real estate investing, as they can have a significant impact on the rental income and potential profits of a property. An accurate appraisal can ensure that a property is priced correctly, making it an essential part of starting a rental real estate company.

Appreciation

Appreciation is an increase in the value of a property over time. This term is important to understand when starting a rental real estate company because investors can use appreciation to increase their equity in a property and generate passive income through rent.

Area Analysis

Area analysis is an evaluation of the location or area where a rental property is located. This includes the evaluation of the neighborhood, crime rate, local amenities, and other factors that affect the desirability of the area. Before starting a rental real estate company, it is essential to conduct a thorough area analysis to ensure that each property is in a suitable location that is attractive to potential tenants.

Assessed Value

Assessed value refers to the value of a property used to determine property taxes. This value is usually lower than the market value of a property and is determined by local government agencies. Investors starting a rental real estate company must be familiar with assessed value because it can affect the amount of property taxes and property insurance premiums, which are significant expenses for rental properties.

Asset

An asset is anything owned by an individual or company that has value. In a rental real estate company, assets include rental properties, land, and equipment. Understanding assets is important because they are the basis of passive income generation.

Benchmarks

Metrics or standards used to measure the performance of a rental real estate business against industry averages or competitors. Common benchmarks include occupancy rates, rent-to-income ratios, net profit margins, and return on investment. Identifying and tracking benchmarks can help owners identify areas for improvement, set goals, and evaluate success.

Bookkeeping

The practice of recording, organizing, and tracking financial transactions related to a rental real estate business. Accurate bookkeeping helps owners keep track of income, expenses, taxes, and cash flow, and prepares them for audits or refinancing.

Brokerage

A firm or agent that facilitates the buying, selling, or renting of real estate properties. Brokers can assist rental property owners with marketing, tenant screening, lease negotiations, and property management.

Budget

The financial plan that outlines the expected income and expenses of a rental real estate company. It includes fixed costs such as mortgage payments, property taxes, and insurance, as well as variable expenses such as maintenance, repairs, and vacancies. A detailed budget helps landlords maximize profits and minimize risks.

Building codes

Local regulations that set standards for the construction, maintenance, and safety of buildings. Rental real estate owners must comply with building codes to avoid penalties, lawsuits, or the risk of tenants getting hurt or sick.

Build-to-rent

A real estate development strategy in which builders construct apartment buildings or single-family homes specifically designed for the rental market. This approach aims to meet the demand for affordable, high-quality rental housing and generate stable rental income for investors.

Business entity

The legal structure under which a rental real estate company operates, such as a sole proprietorship, partnership, LLC, or corporation. Choosing the right business entity can affect liability, taxes, regulation, and ownership structure.

Business license

A permit issued by the local government authorizing a rental real estate company to operate within a specific jurisdiction. Obtaining a business license often involves registering the business name, paying fees, and complying with zoning and safety regulations.

Business plan

A comprehensive written document outlining a rental real estate company's objectives, strategies, target market, financial projections, and marketing tactics. A robust business plan helps rental property owners assess the feasibility of their venture, create a roadmap for growth, and secure funding from investors or lenders.

Buy-and-hold strategy

A long-term investment approach in which rental property owners acquire properties with the intention of holding onto them for several years or decades, while collecting rental income and benefiting from appreciation. This strategy requires careful research, due diligence, and market analysis.

Capital expenditures

Refers to the significant investments made in a rental property that increase its long-term value, such as renovations, repairs, or upgrades. These expenses are typically larger and less frequent than day-to-day operational costs and can impact the cash flow of a rental property.

Cash flow

Refers to the money that is coming in and going out of your rental property. It is important to manage and maintain a positive cash flow, where the income from rent exceeds the expenses involved in running and maintaining the property. This ensures that the rental property is profitable and sustainable in the long run.

Cash reserves

Refers to the amount of money that rental property owners keep on hand to cover unexpected expenses or dips in cash flow. Having a sufficient cash reserve is essential to weather unforeseen events and ensure the financial stability of a rental property.

Cloud-based software

Refers to the online software tools and platforms that rental property owners and managers can use to streamline their business operations. These tools help with various tasks, including rent collection, expense tracking, tenant screening, and maintenance management.

Code compliance

Refers to the local laws and regulations that govern the building and maintenance of a rental property. It includes compliance with safety codes, building codes, fire codes, and accessibility codes. Failure to comply with these rules can result in fines, penalties, or even legal action against the rental property owner.

Communication

Refers to the ability to effectively communicate with tenants, vendors, and other stakeholders involved in the rental property business. Good communication is critical in managing tenant relationships, handling maintenance requests, and resolving disputes.

Community involvement

Refers to the engagement of rental property owners in local communities or neighborhood associations. Engaging with the community can help build positive relationships with tenants, improve the reputation of the rental property, and create opportunities for networking and marketing.

Contingency planning

Refers to the plan for unforeseen events or emergencies that can impact a rental property. This plan should include insurance policies, emergency funds, and protocols for handling issues like natural disasters, tenant evictions, or unexpected vacancies.

Contract agreements

Refers to the legally binding agreements between landlords and tenants, including lease agreements and rental agreements. These documents outline the terms and conditions of the rental arrangement, including the rental amount, payment schedule, security deposit, and any other rules and restrictions.

Credit score

Refers to the numerical representation of an individual's creditworthiness. As a rental property owner, it is essential to screen potential tenants' credit scores to ensure that they have a history of responsible financial behavior and are likely to pay their rent on time.

Damages

Physical harm or loss resulting from a tenant's actions or negligence. If a tenant causes damage to a rental property, the landlord may be entitled to compensation for repair costs or replacement of damaged items. Landlords may require a security deposit to cover potential damages.

Debt Service Coverage Ratio (DSCR)

A financial metric used to evaluate the cash flow of a rental property. DSCR is calculated by dividing the property's net operating income (NOI) by its annual debt payments. A DSCR of less than 1 indicates that the property is not generating enough income to cover its debt payments, while a DSCR of 1 or more indicates that the property is generating enough income to cover its debt payments.

Debt-to-Equity Ratio

A financial metric used to evaluate the financing of a rental property. The debt-to-equity ratio is calculated by dividing the property's total debt by its equity. A lower debt-to-equity ratio indicates that the property is less leveraged and has more equity, which can help reduce financial risk.

Default

The failure to meet the terms of a rental lease agreement or mortgage loan. If a tenant or borrower defaults, the landlord or lender may take legal action to enforce the terms of the agreement, such as eviction or foreclosure.

Deposit

An amount of money paid upfront by a tenant to a landlord at the beginning of a lease. The deposit is usually one month's rent but can be more depending on the landlord's requirements. The deposit provides the landlord with security against any damages caused by the tenant during the lease term. At the end of the lease, the landlord will inspect the property to ensure no damage has been caused and return the deposit amount to the tenant.

Depreciation

A tax deduction that rental property owners can claim for the gradual wear and tear of their property over time. Property depreciation allows owners to reduce their taxable income and save money on taxes. Depreciation is calculated based on the property's value, useful life, and other factors.

Disclosure

The act of sharing information with tenants about the condition of a property or any potential issues that could affect their tenancy. Landlords have a legal obligation to disclose certain information to tenants, such as the presence of lead-based paint or any known defects in the property.

Discrimination

The act of treating people unfairly based on their race, gender, religion, ethnicity, or other personal characteristics. Landlords are legally prohibited from discriminating against tenants based on protected characteristics. Discrimination can come in many forms, including refusing to rent to someone, charging higher rent or fees, or providing different services or treatment to different tenants.

Dual Agency

A situation in which a real estate agent represents both the buyer and the seller in a transaction. Dual agency can create conflicts of interest, as the agent may be unable to provide unbiased advice or negotiate effectively on behalf of either party.

Due Diligence

The process of researching and investigating a property to identify any potential issues or risks that could affect its rental income or value. Due diligence involves reviewing the property's physical condition, financial records, market demand, and legal compliance requirements. Conducting due diligence is essential before purchasing a rental property to ensure its long-term profitability.

Early termination fee

An early termination fee is a fee charged to a tenant who breaks their lease before its expiration date. When drafting lease agreements, it's important to include early termination fee clauses to protect the rental real estate company from financial loss.

Environmental regulations

Environmental regulations refer to laws and guidelines that govern the management and use of natural resources and the impact of human activity on the environment. When operating a rental real estate company, understanding environmental regulations is important for compliance and minimizing any harmful impact on the environment.

Equity

Equity refers to the value of an owner's interest in a property after all debts and liabilities have been paid off. When starting a rental real estate company, understanding equity is important because it can help determine the value of properties and the potential return on investment.

Equity cap

Equity cap is the maximum amount of equity that an investor is willing to invest in a property. When deciding whether or not to invest in a rental property, it's important to consider the equity cap and the potential return on investment.

Equity participation

Equity participation is an investment strategy where an investor provides funding for a rental property in exchange for a share of the property's profits. When starting a rental real estate company, understanding equity participation can provide additional funding for property acquisitions.

Escrow

Escrow is a process where a third party holds onto funds or documents until a specific condition has been met. When purchasing or selling a property, an escrow account is often used to ensure that all parties involved receive their agreed-upon payments and documents.

Eviction

Eviction is the legal process of removing a tenant from a rental property due to non-payment, lease violations, or other reasons. When starting a rental real estate company, it's important to understand the eviction process and the laws governing it in your specific area.

Exclusive listing

An exclusive listing is an agreement between a property owner and a real estate agent where the agent has sole rights to market and sell the property. When starting a rental real estate company, understanding exclusive listings can help determine which properties are available for rent and which are not.

Expense ratio

The expense ratio is the percentage of income from a rental property that is used to cover operating expenses. When evaluating the profitability of a rental property, it's important to consider the expense ratio and ensure that it is sustainable.

Expenses

Expenses refer to the costs associated with owning and managing a rental property, including utilities, maintenance, insurance, and property taxes. Understanding and managing these expenses is crucial for the profitability of a rental real estate company.

Fair Housing Act

A federal law that prohibits discrimination in the sale, rental, and financing of housing based on race, color, religion, sex, national origin, familial status, and disability. Understanding and complying with this law is crucial before starting a rental real estate company to prevent legal issues and discrimination lawsuits.

Fair market rent

The amount of rent that a property can reasonably expect to receive in the current local rental market. This information is crucial for setting the right rent price for a rental property to attract tenants and maximize profits.

Fair wear and tear

The normal deterioration or depreciation that occurs in a rental property due to normal use by tenants. Understanding what constitutes fair wear and tear is crucial when determining whether to charge tenants for damages and how much to charge.

Fiduciary duty

The legal obligation of a landlord to act in the best interests of their tenants and manage the rental property in a responsible and ethical manner. Understanding this duty is crucial before starting a rental real estate company to maintain good relationships with tenants and minimize legal liabilities.

Financing

Obtaining the necessary funds, such as loans or mortgage, to purchase and manage rental properties. Understanding the different financing options, interest rates, and terms is essential before starting a rental real estate company.

Fire safety

Ensuring that rental properties meet the fire safety codes and standards set by the local government, such as having working smoke detectors, fire extinguishers, and fire escape plans. Failure to comply with fire safety regulations can result in severe penalties, injury, or loss of life, making it a critical aspect to consider when starting a rental real estate company.

Fixed expenses

The regular expenses that occur regardless of occupancy rate, such as insurance, property taxes, and maintenance fees. Knowing the fixed expenses is important when analyzing the profitability of a rental property and setting rental rates.

Fixed-term lease

A rental agreement that specifies a set period of time, such as one year or six months. This lease provides stability and predictability for both the landlord and tenants and helps prevent conflicts and misunderstandings.

Forms and contracts

Legal documents that specify the terms and conditions of the rental agreement, such as lease agreement, rental application, eviction notice, and security deposit agreement. Properly drafting and executing these forms and contracts is important to protect the rights and interests of both parties.

Furnished vs. unfurnished

Choosing whether to rent furnished or unfurnished properties can significantly affect the rental income and expenses, as well as attract different types of renters. It's important to consider the demand, competition, and cost before deciding on the type of rental property.

Good Faith Deposit

A sum of money paid by a prospective tenant to the landlord before the lease agreement is signed. This provides assurance to the landlord that the tenant is committed to renting the property, and can be used to cover expenses if the tenant defaults before moving in.

Grievance Procedure

A formal process established to resolve disputes between tenants and landlords. This may involve filing complaints with government agencies, seeking mediation, or pursuing legal action.

Gross Income Ratio

A calculation that compares the rental income of a property to its total expenses. This is useful in determining the profitability of a rental property and whether it can generate sufficient income to cover its expenses.

Gross Lease

A type of lease agreement in which the tenant pays a fixed amount of rent and the landlord is responsible for all property expenses, such as taxes, insurance, and maintenance. This is in contrast to a triple net lease, where the tenant is responsible for these expenses.

Gross Potential Rent

The total potential income a rental property could generate if all units were rented out at market rates without any vacancies or delinquencies. This figure assumes perfect market conditions.

Gross Rent Multiplier

A ratio used to determine the value of a rental property based on the amount of gross rental income it generates. The gross rent multiplier is calculated by dividing the property's purchase price by its gross rental income.

Gross Rental Income

The total amount of income generated by a rental property before any expenses are deducted. This includes rent payments and any other income sources, such as laundry facilities or parking fees.

Ground Rent

An annual fee paid by the leaseholder to the freeholder for the right to use and occupy the land on which the property is built. Ground rent is typically found in leasehold arrangements and can increase over time.

Guarantor

A person or entity who assumes responsibility for a tenant's financial obligations in the event that the tenant defaults on rent or damages the property. A guarantor is often required for tenants with bad credit or low income.

Guest

A person who is not listed on the lease agreement but stays in the rental property temporarily with the permission of the tenant or landlord. Local laws may dictate the length of stay allowed for guests and the responsibilities of tenants and landlords in hosting guests.

Hard Money Loans

Refers to a type of loan that is secured by real estate. These loans are often used by real estate investors to purchase fix-and-flip properties or other investment properties. Hard money loans typically have higher interest rates and shorter repayment terms than traditional loans, and they often require a significant down payment.

Hazard Insurance

Refers to insurance that covers damage or loss due to various hazards, such as fire, theft, and natural disasters. This is an important type of insurance for rental properties, as it can protect the landlord's investment and provide peace of mind to tenants. It is important to shop around for the best rates and coverage when purchasing hazard insurance for a rental property.

HOA Dues

Refers to the monthly fees paid by members of a homeowners association. These fees are used to cover the costs of common area maintenance, landscaping, and other services. It is important to understand the HOA dues when purchasing a property that is part of an HOA, as they can significantly impact the property's overall expenses.

Holding Costs

Refers to the expenses incurred while holding onto a property, such as mortgage payments, property taxes, and utility bills. These costs are important to factor in when determining rental rates and can significantly impact profits. It is important to keep track of these expenses and budget accordingly to ensure that the rental income covers the holding costs.

Home Equity

The difference between the value of a property and the outstanding balance on any mortgages or liens. This can be a valuable asset for real estate investors, as it can be used to finance additional property purchases or make improvements to existing properties. It is important to understand the equity in a property before using it as collateral or leveraging it for other investments.

Home Inspection

A thorough examination of a property's physical condition, including its roof, foundation, plumbing, electrical, and HVAC systems. This is an important step before purchasing a rental property, as it can reveal hidden defects and potential maintenance issues. A proper home inspection can help investors make informed decisions and avoid costly repairs.

Home Warranty

A service contract that covers the repair and replacement of certain home appliances and systems. This can be a valuable asset for rental properties, as it can provide peace of mind to tenants and reduce the landlord's maintenance costs.

Homeowners Association (HOA)

A group responsible for enforcing rules, regulations, and standards in a particular community or complex. When purchasing a property that is part of an HOA, it is important to understand the fees, regulations, and obligations involved. These fees can vary greatly, and failure to comply with the HOA's regulations can result in fines and legal action.

Housing Market

The overall supply and demand for housing in a particular area. Understanding the housing market is crucial for real estate investors, as it can impact rental rates and property values. Factors such as population growth, job opportunities, and interest rates all play a role in the housing market.

Human Resources

Refers to the management of employees in a rental real estate company. This includes hiring, training, and managing employees, as well as handling employee benefits, payroll, and legal compliance. Having a strong human resources department can help ensure the success of a rental real estate company.

Income Property

An income property is a real estate property that generates income through renting or leasing out the property. Before starting a rental real estate company, it's important to consider the type of income property you want to invest in, such as residential, commercial, or industrial properties.

Inspection

An inspection is a thorough examination of the rental property to identify any potential issues or damages. Inspections are important for both the landlord and the tenant as it ensures the property is in good condition and any needed repairs are addressed before new tenants move in.

Insurance

This refers to a policy that covers damages to the rental property. It's important to have insurance to protect your assets and avoid financial loss. Different types of insurance include liability insurance, property insurance, and rental income coverage insurance.

Investment Property

An investment property is a property purchased with the goal of generating income or profit, typically through renting or leasing. Before starting a rental real estate company, it's important to have a clear investment strategy and consider factors such as location, rental demand, and property condition.

Joint Account

A joint account is a bank account that is shared by two or more individuals, each of whom has equal access and responsibility for the account. This can be useful for rental real estate companies that need to manage shared expenses or rents between multiple owners or partners.

Joint and Several Liability

Joint and several liability refers to a legal concept in which multiple parties may be held responsible for the same debt or obligation. This can be relevant for a rental real estate company, as co-owners or partners may be held jointly and severally liable for any debts or damages incurred by the company.

Joint Commission

The Joint Commission is an independent organization that accredits healthcare facilities and programs in the United States. While not directly related to rental real estate, understanding the standards and requirements set forth by the Joint Commission can be helpful for companies that operate in healthcare or medical real estate.

Joint Lease

A joint lease is a type of lease agreement in which multiple tenants are jointly responsible for paying rent and fulfilling other lease obligations. This can be useful for rental properties with multiple tenants or roommates.

Joint Tenancy

Joint tenancy is a type of property ownership where two or more individuals own the property together, with equal rights to the property. When one joint tenant dies, their share of the property automatically passes to the surviving joint tenants. This can be helpful for a rental real estate company, as it can simplify the process of transferring ownership of a property between owners.

Joint Venture

A joint venture is a business agreement in which two or more parties agree to work together on a specific project or venture. In a rental real estate context, this might involve partnering with another company or individual to acquire, develop, or manage a property.

Judgment

A judgment is a decision made by a court or legal system, typically following a lawsuit or legal dispute. As a rental real estate company, it is important to be aware of any judgments against your company or your properties, as these can impact your ability to operate or finance your business.

Jumbo loan

A jumbo loan is a type of mortgage loan that exceeds the conforming loan limits set by Fannie Mae and Freddie Mac. These loans are typically used for higher-priced properties or investment properties. As a rental real estate company, it is important to be aware of jumbo loan options when financing property purchases or renovations.

Jurisdiction

Jurisdiction refers to the geographic area in which a specific court or legal system has power. As a rental real estate company, it is important to understand the jurisdiction in which your properties are located, as different areas may have specific laws or regulations that impact your operations.

Jurisprudence

Jurisprudence refers to the study or philosophy of law, including the history, concepts, and principles behind legal systems. While not directly applicable to a rental real estate company, a basic understanding of jurisprudence can be helpful for navigating legal issues and disputes in the industry.

Keep accurate financial records

Financial record-keeping is crucial to the longevity of your business. Be sure to record all expenses, rental income, and other financial transactions, and keep all receipts and invoices. This will allow you to track your success and also make tax filing much easier.

Key money

A term used to describe a lump sum of money paid by a tenant to a landlord, often in addition to rent and as a condition for being allowed to rent the property. Key money is becoming increasingly uncommon due to the fact that it can be seen as illegal and unethical.

Key performance indicators

KPI's are used to evaluate the success of a rental real estate company. Track important metrics like occupancy rates, average rental rate, and rental income to identify areas of success and target areas for improvement.

Key rental terms

Familiarize yourself with key rental terms like security deposit, late rent fees, and rental insurance. Efficient communication with tenants and prompt handling of all rental related matters will greatly benefit both you and the tenants.

Kitchen and bathroom quality

The quality and state of the kitchen and bathrooms can greatly affect the rental value of your property. Upgrading and maintaining these areas should be a priority to attract potential tenants and ensure their satisfaction with the property.

Kitting out your rental property

Furnishing your rental property is a critical part of attracting tenants and ensuring their comfortability. Consider investing in essential furniture such as beds, couches, and desks, and ensure the appliances like washing machines, fridges, and microwaves are in good working conditions. Offering more comfortable and well-maintained properties with amenities can help you to obtain higher rental fees in the long run.

Knowledge of local and state laws

Real estate laws can be complex and vary depending on the state or even the city in which you are investing. It is important to do thorough research and familiarize yourself with these laws to ensure that you are operating within legal boundaries. Not doing so can result in fines, lawsuits, or even lose your investment entirely.

Knowledge of property management

Property management is a crucial aspect of a rental real estate company. Ensure you have a strong understanding of tenant screening, lease agreements, maintenance, and repairs, and the legal obligations of landlords.

Knowledge of property taxes

Property taxes can vary greatly depending on the property and location. It is important to understand the tax implications of owning a rental property, what expenses can be claimed and what can't be claimed.

Knowledge of the rental market

Knowing the current trends and conditions of the rental real estate market in your chosen location will help you decide property value, rental rates, and even rental terms. Keep a lookout for market shifts, both positive and negative, and adjust your business strategy accordingly.

Landlord Insurance

Insurance that protects the landlord from risks associated with their rental property, such as damage caused by tenants or natural disasters. It is different from homeowner's insurance because it covers rental activities such as liability claims involving tenants and rental income loss.

Landlord-tenant Law

The set of laws that govern the relationship between landlords and tenants, including the rights and obligations of both parties. It covers areas such as lease agreement formation and requirements, eviction processes and fair housing practices.

Late Fee

A fee charged by the landlord when the tenant fails to pay rent on time. The amount and terms of the fee must be specified in the lease agreement.

Lead Paint Disclosure

Federal law requires landlords to inform tenants about the presence of lead-based paint in homes built before 1978. This disclosure must be provided to tenants before the lease is signed, allowing them to make an informed decision about whether to rent the property.

Lead Paint Poisoning

A serious health condition resulting from exposure to lead-based paint. Landlords are required by law to disclose the presence of lead-based paint in homes built before 1978 and must take measures to remove or cover it if it poses a health risk to tenants.

Lease Agreement

A legally binding document that outlines the terms and conditions of the rental agreement between the landlord and the tenant. It specifies the rent to be paid, the duration of the lease, the security deposit and other terms such as the use of the property, late payment or breach of contract remedies.

Lease Renewal

The process of extending the lease term when the initial lease agreement is about to expire. It typically involves negotiating new terms and a new rental rate for the continued use of the rental property.

Leasehold Improvements

Changes made to a rental property by the tenant to suit their specific needs or business requirements. It can include things such as customized flooring, additional lighting or electrical outlets, and may require landlord approval before installation.

Letter of Intent

A written statement outlining the intentions of the landlord or tenant's interest in leasing a property. It is not a legally binding agreement, but it can help to facilitate negotiations between the parties.

Loss of Use Coverage

Insurance coverage provided to landlords that reimburses them for lost rental income when a rental property becomes uninhabitable due to damages covered by insurance, such as fire or water damage. It can be purchased as part of a landlord insurance policy.

Maintenance

Refers to the upkeep and repair of rental property units. Regular maintenance helps attract tenants, retain them, and increase property value. Maintenance involves preventive measures, such as cleaning, painting, and inspecting equipment, as well as fix and repair of damage.

Maintenance Reserve Funds

A set-aside amount of money that rental property owners keep for unexpected repairs, upgrades, and maintenance. It is important to have a fund in place to ensure the property continues to generate revenue even if rental activities slow down.

Management Plan

A comprehensive outline of the policies, procedures, rules, and goals of the rental real estate company. The management plan is designed to ensure the property is well run, and the needs of its stakeholders, such as investors, renters, and staff, are addressed.

Market Analysis

A critical tool that helps real estate companies identify and evaluate viable rental markets. Through market analysis, companies can determine current and future market trends, predict demand and occupancy rates, and thus decide the best area to invest their resources.

Market Rent

The rental rate that a property can generate based on the current market conditions, competition, location, and other factors. Understanding this term helps rental real estate owners set realistic rental prices for their properties and capitalize on market opportunities.

Marketing strategy

The overall plan to attract renters to your rental real estate property. Examples include advertising in local publications, word of mouth, digital marketing, etc. It is important to develop a targeted marketing strategy as it can significantly affect the rental rate and occupancy rate of the property.

Master Lease Agreement

A legal document that allows the rental property owner to lease all or part of their property to a third party. The third party, called the "master tenant," can then sublet the space to other tenants. This agreement can create added revenue streams for owners and attract long-term tenants.

Mortgage

A legal agreement that enables individuals or companies to borrow money from a financial institution to finance their rental property investments. It is essential to understand the various types of mortgages, their interest rates, and the cost of down payments.

Move-in Checklist

A list of items and conditions that tenants have to review and confirm before moving into the rental property. It is a crucial document to determine the condition of the property before and after the rental period.

Multifamily Property

A property that has more than one dwelling unit, for example, apartments, duplexes, condos, or townhouses.

National Apartment Association (NAA)

A national trade association representing landlords, property managers, and other professionals in the rental housing industry. NAA provides education, advocacy, and networking opportunities to its members and serves as a voice for the industry's interests.

National Association of Residential Property Managers (NARPM)

A professional organization that serves as a resource for residential property managers, landlords, and their clients. NARPM offers educational programs, professional designations, and networking opportunities to its members.

National Real Estate Investors Association (NREIA)

A non-profit organization formed to provide a platform for real estate investors to share knowledge and resources, network, and advance the industry's interests. NREIA members have access to educational seminars, networking events, and vendor discounts. Joining a local NREIA chapter can help rental property business owners learn the local real estate market and build valuable relationships with other investors.

Net Cash Flow

The cash flow generated by a rental property after all operating expenses, debts, and taxes have been paid. Net cash flow is a crucial metric to evaluate the profitability of any rental property investment opportunity. Investors use net cash flow to determine if a property will generate positive or negative returns.

Net Leased Investment Property

A type of commercial real estate that entails a long-term lease agreement between the property owner and a tenant. The tenant is responsible for most of the property expenses, such as maintenance, repairs, insurance, and taxes. Net leased properties offer stable and predictable income streams for the investors.

Net Operating Income (NOI)

Represents the potential rental income minus operating expenses, excluding debt service. NOI is a significant metric to evaluate the profitability of a rental property. Knowing the property NOI helps the investor determine whether a rental property is a good investment that can generate cash flow over time.

Niche Market

A sub-segment of a market that targets a specific customer group with particular needs, preferences, or characteristics. In rental real estate, niche markets can include college rentals, vacation rentals, or assisted living facilities. Targeting a niche market can help rental property business owners differentiate themselves from the competition and pursue unique investment opportunities.

Non-Compete Agreement

A legal agreement that prohibits an individual or company from competing with another party for a specified period or within a specific geographic location. Non-compete agreements are essential for rental real estate businesses to ensure their employees or contractors do not start similar businesses or work for the competition.

Non-Disclosure Agreement (NDA)

A legally binding agreement between two or more parties that aims to protect confidential information from being disclosed to third parties. NDAs are essential in rental real estate businesses to protect trade secrets, client data, and proprietary information.

Non-Recourse Loan

A loan arrangement that does not hold the borrower personally liable for the loan repayment. In rental real estate, non-recourse loans are common for commercial properties and multifamily dwellings. Non-recourse loans limit the borrower's liability in case of default or foreclosure.

Occupancy Cost

Refers to the total cost of leasing a rental property, including monthly rent, utilities, maintenance fees, and any other expenses associated with occupancy. Understanding and managing occupancy costs is important in setting rents, negotiating leases, and maintaining profitability for rental real estate companies.

Occupancy Rates

Refers to the percentage of rental units that are currently being rented out in a particular location or community. This can be influenced by a variety of factors including local economic conditions, demand for housing, competition from other rental properties, and the availability of rental units. Understanding occupancy rates is crucial to the success of a rental real estate company as it helps to determine pricing, marketing strategies, and overall profitability. High occupancy rates are generally desirable as they indicate a high demand for rental properties and can lead to increased revenue and stability in the market.

Off-Market Properties

Refers to rental properties that are not publicly listed for sale or rent. These properties may be available to investors and rental real estate companies through private networks, referrals, or other means. Off-market properties can provide unique investment opportunities with favorable terms, but may require additional effort and networking to identify and acquire.

Operating Agreement

Refers to a legal document that outlines the ownership structure, management responsibilities, and operating procedures of a rental real estate company. Operating agreements are typically used for LLCs (limited liability companies) and help to establish clear guidelines for decision-making, profit distribution, and other important aspects of company governance.

Operating Expenses

Refers to the costs associated with maintaining and operating a rental property such as property taxes, insurance, repairs, utilities, and property management fees. These expenses can often be significant and must be factored into the overall financial analysis of a rental property. Understanding and minimizing operating expenses is key to maximizing profitability and ensuring the long-term success of a rental real estate company.

Opportunity Cost

Refers to the potential return on investment that is foregone as a result of choosing one option over another. In the context of rental real estate, opportunity cost may arise when choosing between different investment opportunities or strategies. Understanding opportunity cost is important in evaluating the potential returns and risks associated with different investment options.

Original Lease Term

Refers to the period of time specified in a lease agreement during which a tenant is obligated to occupy and pay rent for a rental property. The original lease term can impact the potential profitability of an investment property, as longer leases may provide greater stability and predictability, while shorter leases offer more flexibility.

Outsourcing

Refers to the practice of hiring external firms or professionals to handle certain aspects of a rental real estate company's operations, such as property management or bookkeeping. Outsourcing can reduce costs, improve efficiency, and allow rental real estate companies to focus on their core competencies.

Overhead

Refers to the ongoing fixed costs of running a rental real estate company such as office rent, utilities, equipment, and insurance. These costs are distinct from operating expenses which are directly related to the maintenance and operation of rental properties. Effective management of overhead is critical to ensuring the financial health and profitability of a rental real estate company.

Owner Financing

Refers to a financing arrangement in which the seller of a property agrees to finance all or part of the purchase price for the buyer. This can be an attractive option for buyers who may not qualify for traditional financing, and can also provide benefits to the seller in the form of additional income and a quicker sale.

Partnership

A joint business venture between two or more entities. A partnership can provide additional resources and expertise to a rental real estate company, as well as splitting the risks and costs associated with property ownership and management.

Performance Metrics

Data points that determine the effectiveness of a rental real estate company. These can include vacancy rates, rent collection rates, tenant retention rates, and maintenance costs.

Permits and Licenses

The legal requirements necessary to operate a rental real estate company, including business licenses, permits for property renovations or additions, and compliance with zoning and housing regulations. Failure to obtain the necessary licenses and permits can result in hefty fines and legal issues.

Portfolio

A collection of rental properties owned by a real estate company. This can include residential or commercial properties, and each property is an asset in the company's investment portfolio.

Professional Network

A group of industry professionals who can provide valuable insight, expertise and connections to help a rental real estate company grow and thrive. This network can include real estate agents, attorneys, accountants, and contractors.

Profit Margin

The difference between the revenue earned from rental properties and the expenses of operating and maintaining those properties. A rental real estate company must aim for a high profit margin to be sustainable and successful.

Property Inspection

A thorough assessment of a rental property that identifies any necessary repairs or maintenance to ensure the property is safe and habitable for tenants. Regular inspections can prevent costly repairs and keep tenants satisfied.

Property Management

The process of overseeing the operations, maintenance, and administration of a rental property portfolio. This includes handling tenant applications, rent collection, property maintenance and repairs, and ensuring compliance with housing laws and regulations. Effective property management is essential for the success of a rental real estate company.

Property Tax

A tax paid on the value of a rental property that goes towards local government services such as schools and emergency services. It's important for a rental real estate company to consider property taxes as an expense when calculating the potential profitability of a property investment.

Property Valuation

The process of estimating the value of a rental property. This is important to ensure that the property is priced appropriately for rental income and to determine the potential return on investment.

Real estate market analysis

The process of evaluating the local real estate market to determine the supply and demand for rental properties. This includes researching the area's rental rates, vacancy rates, and population growth trends. Analyzing the local real estate market can help rental property investors identify potential investment opportunities and mitigate risks.

Rent control

A policy that limits the amount of rent that landlords can charge for their rental properties. Rent control laws vary by state and local jurisdiction, and compliance is important for rental property owners to avoid legal issues and penalties.

Rental agreement

A legal document that outlines the terms and conditions of a rental agreement between a landlord and tenant. The rental agreement should specify the rent amount, lease term, security deposit amount, and any other important provisions or policies. Having a clearly written rental agreement is important for protecting both the landlord and tenant's rights.

Rental application

A document that prospective tenants complete when applying for a rental property. It typically includes information such as the tenant's employment history, credit score, and references. As a landlord, using a rental application can help you screen tenants and make informed decisions about who to rent to.

Rental property

A property that is owned by a landlord and is available for rent to tenants. Before starting a rental real estate company, it is important to determine the type of rental property you want to invest in, such as apartments, single-family homes, or commercial buildings. Understanding the market demand and rental rates in your target location is also critical to making informed investment decisions.

Rental property insurance

Insurance that covers rental property owners in the event of property damage, liability claims, and loss of rental income. Landlords should obtain adequate insurance coverage to protect their investment and mitigate financial risk.

Rental property management

The process of overseeing the day-to-day operations of a rental property, including tenant screening, rent collection, maintenance, and repairs. Before starting a rental real estate company, it is important to evaluate whether you will handle property management in-house or outsource it to a third-party management company.

Rental property tax deductions

Tax deductions that landlords can claim on their rental property expenses, such as mortgage interest, property taxes, and maintenance costs. Before starting a rental real estate company, it is important to understand the tax implications of owning rental properties and work with a qualified accountant to ensure compliance with tax laws.

Rental yield

This is the income generated from a rental property relative to its investment cost. It is calculated by dividing the annual rental income by the property's value. As a real estate investor, understanding the rental yield of a property can help you determine its potential profitability and compare it to other investment opportunities.

Rent-to-income ratio

This ratio compares the rental income of a property to the income of the tenants who live there. It is an important metric to consider when deciding how much rent to charge, as well as determining the financial feasibility of a rental property investment. Typically, acceptable rent-to-income ratios range from 30-40%.

Schedule Maintenance

The process of planning regular maintenance and repairs on the rental property to ensure that it is in good condition. Landlords must schedule maintenance based on the tenant's convenience and comply with state and federal laws. Proper maintenance can help prevent serious maintenance issues that may be costly in the long run.

Screening Criteria

The specific requirements that a potential tenant must meet to be accepted for the rental property. These criteria vary by property and landlord but typically include factors such as income, credit history, rental history, and criminal record. The landlord must establish reasonable screening criteria that are not discriminatory to avoid legal issues.

Screening Process

The process of vetting potential tenants to ensure that only the most suitable ones are accepted for the rental property. Property managers typically assess the tenant's credit history, rental history, employment status, and criminal background. The screening process is necessary to avoid evictions and legal disputes that may arise from unsuitable tenants.

Security Cameras

A system of video cameras installed on the rental property to monitor security and deter criminal activity. While security cameras may be an added expense, they can help prevent property damage or theft and provide legal evidence in case of a dispute.

Security Deposit

A sum of money paid by the tenant to the landlord at the beginning of the lease term to cover any potential damages to the rental property or unpaid rent. The security deposit amount varies by state and landlord but is usually equal to one or two months' rent. It is crucial for the landlord to know the rules and regulations regarding security deposits in their state to avoid any legal issues.

Serve Notice

The act of formally notifying the tenant of a lease violation, rent increase or any other issue that requires their attention. The notice should be in writing and comply with state and federal laws. The timing and method of serving notice may also vary by state or city, so landlords must know the regulations in their area.

Standard Lease Agreement

A legal document that outlines the terms and conditions of the rental agreement. It includes details such as the rental amount, security deposit, lease length, maintenance responsibilities, and late fees. The landlord can customize the lease agreement to fit the specific needs of their rental property but must comply with state and federal laws.

Standard Operating Procedures

A set of guidelines and processes that landlords follow, such as rent collection or move-in procedures. Standard operating procedures help landlords ensure consistency in property management, avoid mistakes or oversights, and provide better service to tenants. Landlords may customize the SOP based on their rental property and tenant's needs.

State Landlord-Tenant Laws

A set of rules and regulations that govern the relationship between the landlord and the tenant. They cover areas such as security deposits, rent increases, eviction procedures, and tenant rights. Understanding these laws is essential for landlords to avoid legal issues and ensure that they are complying with the law.

Subletting

The act of renting out a rental property to another tenant other than the original tenant. Before allowing subletting, landlords must review their lease agreement, state landlord-tenant laws, and consult with their legal counsel. Subletting may cause legal issues or property damages if not done correctly, so landlords must be cautious.

Tax deductions

As a rental property owner, tax deductions can significantly reduce your taxable income, including mortgage interest, property taxes, insurance, repairs, and maintenance expenses.

Team building

Developing a reliable team of contractors, property managers, real estate agents, and other professionals can help rental property owners to streamline their operations, improve their services, and increase their profits. Building a strong network of individuals who share your values and work ethic can be invaluable in growing your rental real estate company.

Tenant lease agreement

A legally binding document that outlines the terms and conditions of a rental agreement between a landlord and a tenant, including rent payments, security deposits, pet policies, maintenance responsibilities, and eviction procedures.

Tenant retention

The act of keeping good tenants happy and renewing their lease by providing quality customer service, timely repairs, and upgrades to the property.

Tenant rights

The legal protections and entitlements given to tenants, such as the right to a habitable living space, privacy, and protection against discrimination, eviction, and retaliation.

Tenant screening

A crucial process of selecting tenants for your rental property that involves checking their credit history, employment status, references, and criminal records. This helps landlords to lower the risk of renting to unreliable or dangerous tenants.

Tenant turnover

The process of a tenant leaving a property, and the landlord preparing the property for a new tenant, which includes cleaning, repairs, maintenance, and advertising.

Time management

Effective time management skills are essential for rental property owners to manage the day-to-day operations of a rental business, including screening tenants, responding to maintenance requests, and keeping up with paperwork.

Title search

A search of public records done to verify legal ownership of a property, identify any liens or easements, and ensure the property has a clear title before purchasing it.

Trust account

A separate bank account used to hold security deposits, rent payments, or other funds related to a rental property. It's essential to maintain accurate records of all transactions in the trust account to comply with legal and accounting requirements.

Uncollected Rent

Uncollected rent refers to the rent payments that tenants fail to pay on time or at all. Uncollected rent can be due to various reasons, such as tenants losing their jobs, disputes with landlords, or changes in their financial circumstances. Rental property owners should have a plan in place for collecting uncollected rent, such as issuing late payment notices or eviction proceedings.

Underwriting

Underwriting refers to the process of evaluating the potential risks and benefits of a rental property investment. This process involves analyzing factors such as the rental income potential of the property, local real estate market conditions, and future maintenance costs. Underwriting helps investors tailor their rental real estate business plans to maximize profitability and minimize risks.

Uniform Residential Landlord and Tenant Act (URLTA)

The URLTA is a set of standardized laws that help regulate the relationship between landlords and tenants. It covers essential areas such as security deposits, lease agreements, and property maintenance. These laws vary by state but serve as a helpful guide for all rental property owners.

Unit Mix

The unit mix refers to the number of different types of rental units (such as studios, one-bedroom, or two-bedroom apartments) available in a rental property. The unit mix can impact the rental income potential of the property, as some unit types may be more popular or in demand than others. It is crucial to balance the unit mix carefully to ensure maximum rental income and tenant occupancy.

Upgrades

Upgrades are improvements made to a rental property to increase its value, appeal, and functionality. Upgrades can include adding new appliances, upgrading fixtures, and installing modern finishes. These can help increase the property's rental price and attract more high-quality tenants. It is crucial to assess the cost versus rental income potential of upgrades beforehand to avoid overcapitalization.

Upkeep

In the rental real estate business, upkeep refers to the ongoing maintenance and repair of a rental property. Upkeep can include tasks such as landscaping, cleaning, and fixing repairs. Proper upkeep is essential to preserving the property's value, reducing vacancy periods, and avoiding tenant dissatisfaction due to poor property maintenance.

Uptime

Uptime refers to the amount of time that a rental property is operational and available for tenant occupancy. Uptime is affected by various factors like maintenance schedules, tenant turnover rates, and emergency repairs. Maximizing uptime is crucial to ensuring a property achieves its full rental income potential and avoids income loss due to vacancy periods.

Usury Laws

Usury laws are state-level laws that regulate the maximum amount of interest landlords can charge tenants. These laws help protect tenants from exorbitant interest rates and predatory lending practices. Rental property owners must be familiar with state-level usury laws and ensure their leases comply with these laws.

Utility Costs

The expenses incurred in the provision of services to rental properties such as electricity, gas, water, and trash collection are commonly known as utility costs. These costs can have a significant impact on your overall rental property profitability. The amount of utility costs can vary depending on the location and size of your property. It is important to include these costs in your rental agreement to avoid disputes with tenants over who is responsible for paying these costs.

Utility Management

Utility management refers to the process of managing all of the utility services and expenses associated with a rental property, such as gas, water, and electricity. Effective utility management involves budgeting for these expenses, managing tenant usage, and making energy-efficient upgrades to reduce costs over time. Proper utility management can help minimize expenses and maximize rental income potential.

Vacancy Rate

The percentage of rental units that are unoccupied at a particular time. This is an important metric to track as a high vacancy rate can negatively impact your rental income and cash flow. A low vacancy rate indicates a healthy demand for rental properties in your area, while a high vacancy rate may require adjusting rental prices or marketing efforts to fill vacant units.

Vacancy-Adjusted Net Operating Income (VAN)

A tool used in property valuation that considers the potential rental income of a property while accounting for vacancies and other associated expenses. VAN can be used to assess the viability of a rental property and forecast future returns based on different occupancy and rental rate scenarios. It's an essential metric to monitor when establishing and adjusting rental rates to ensure positive cash flow and profitability.

Vacate Notice

A written notice served by a tenant indicating their intention to vacate the rental property on a certain date. Vacate notices should be reviewed carefully to determine the dates the tenants will move out, and to allow sufficient time to prepare the rental for the next tenant. This notice can also serve as an opportunity to collect tenant feedback on their rental experience and gather recommendations for improving your rental business.

vacation rental

Properties rented out for short-term stays, typically for periods of less than 30 days. Vacation rentals can offer a potentially higher return on investment compared to long-term rentals, but can also require more management, marketing, and maintenance effort due to the constant turnover of renters.

Vendor Management

The process of managing and maintaining relationships with vendors and contractors who help maintain or repair your rental properties. This includes selecting and sourcing vendors, negotiating service agreements and tracking vendor performance. Effective vendor management can help maintain the value and quality of your rental properties while minimizing maintenance costs and maximizing tenant satisfaction.

Verification of Income

The process of verifying the income of potential renters. This can include reviewing pay stubs, tax returns or contacting an employer directly. Verifying renters' income can help ensure that they can afford the monthly rent and any associated fees. It's important to establish a standard policy for verification of income to help maintain consistency and compliance with anti-discrimination laws.

Verification of Rental History

The process of verifying the rental history of potential tenants, typically through contacting prior landlords or property management companies. Verification of rental history can provide valuable information on a tenant's payment history, behavior, and other relevant details that can affect their suitability as a renter.

Vinyl Flooring

A type of flooring made from synthetic materials like PVC, which is popular in rental properties due to its durability and relatively low cost. Vinyl flooring comes in many colors and styles, mimicking the look of other popular types of flooring such as hardwood or tile. This flooring option is easy to clean and maintain, making it a great choice for high traffic areas in rental properties.

Virtual Tours

A way to showcase your rental properties online without requiring physical in-person showings. Virtual tours can be conducted through various media, such as 3D videos, panoramic photos or live, remote tours conducted over a video conferencing platform. Virtual tours can be an effective tool to attract out-of-state renters or to eliminate unnecessary in-person showings.

Voids and Turnover

The amount of time between one tenant moving out and the next tenant moving in. Voids and turnover can impact your rental income; the longer the property remains vacant, the bigger the financial loss. Effective marketing and tenant screening can help reduce voids and minimize the time it takes to prepare the rental for the next tenant.

Waiver

A legal document that releases a party from any claims or rights. In the context of rental real estate, the landlord may ask the tenant to sign a waiver stating that they are aware of any potential hazards on the property and release the landlord from liability.

Walkthrough inspection

A visual examination of a rental property conducted by both the landlord and tenant at the beginning and end of the lease period. The purpose of the inspection is to identify any existing damages or issues that may arise during the tenancy.

Warrant of habitability

A document issued by a local government agency certifying that a rental property is safe and meets minimum health and safety standards. Landlords must comply with these standards before offering the rental property to tenants.

Warranty of fitness

A guarantee that a rental property is suitable for the intended purpose of living. Landlords must ensure that their rental properties are safe and habitable, and provide a living environment with adequate amenities such as heating, water, and electricity.

Water damage insurance

An insurance policy that provides coverage for water damage caused by unexpected leaks, floods, or storms. Landlords must purchase this insurance to protect their rental properties from water damage.

Wear and tear

The normal and expected damage that occurs to a rental property over time due to regular use. The landlord is responsible for maintaining the property and repairing any damages caused by wear and tear, while the tenant is responsible for damages caused by negligence or misuse.

Website listing

An online listing of a rental property with details such as location, amenities, price, and contact information. This is a common marketing tool used by landlords to attract potential tenants and promote their rental properties.

Withdrawal

The act of a landlord canceling an offer for a rental property before it is accepted by a tenant. This can occur for various reasons, including the landlord's desire to rent the property to someone else or not rent it out at all.

Writ of possession

A legal document that orders a tenant to vacate a rental property. This is typically issued by a court after the landlord has obtained a judgment for eviction due to non-payment of rent or other lease violations.

Written lease agreement

A legal document that outlines the terms and conditions of the rental agreement between the landlord and tenant. This includes details about rent payments, security deposits, repairs and maintenance, and other important provisions.